WELCOME TO THE U.S.A.
RHODE ISLAND

Written by Ann Heinrichs   Illustrated by Matt Kania
Content Adviser: Karen Eberhart, Historical Consultant,
Providence, Rhode Island

The Child's World

Published in the United States of America by The Child's World®
PO Box 326 • Chanhassen, MN 55317-0326
800-599-READ • www.childsworld.com

Photo Credits
Cover: Providence Warwick Convention and Visitors Bureau; frontispiece:
Providence Warwick Convention and Visitors Bureau.

Interior: AP/Wide World: 10 (Stew Milne), 25 (Joe Giblin), 29 (Victoria Arocho),
34 (Westerly Sun/Daniel Hyland); Corbis: 6 (Bob Krist), 9 (W. Wisniewski), 17
(Lee Snider/Photo Images), 23 (Bettmann), 26 (Catherine Karnow), 30 (Kelly-
Mooney Photography); Gaspée Days Committee: 21; Jamestown Yacht Club: 33;
Preservation Society of Newport County: 14; Slater Mill Historic Site: 22; Smith's
Castle: 13; South County Museum: 18.

Acknowledgments
The Child's World®: Mary Berendes, Publishing Director

Editorial Directions, Inc.: E. Russell Primm, Editorial Director; Katie Marsico, Associate
Editor; Judith Shiffer, Assistant Editor; Matt Messbarger, Editorial Assistant; Susan
Hindman, Copy Editor; Melissa McDaniel, Proofreader; Kevin Cunningham, Peter
Garnham, Matt Messbarger, Olivia Nellums, Chris Simms,
Molly Symmonds, Katherine Trickle, Carl Stephen Wender, Fact Checkers; Tim Griffin/
IndexServ, Indexer; Cian Loughlin O'Day, Photo Researcher and Editor

The Design Lab: Kathleen Petelinsek, Design; Julia Goozen, Art Production

Library of Congress Cataloging-in-Publication Data
Heinrichs, Ann.
  Rhode Island / by Ann Heinrichs ; cartography and illustrations by Matt Kania.
    p. cm. — (Welcome to the U.S.A.)
  Includes index.
  ISBN 1-59296-481-8 (library bound : alk. paper) 1. Rhode Island—Juvenile literature.
I. Kania, Matt, ill. II. Title.
  F79.3.H4563 2006
  974.5—dc22   2005009092

**About the Author
Ann Heinrichs**

Ann Heinrichs is the author of more than 100 books for children and young adults. She has also enjoyed successful careers as a children's book editor and an advertising copywriter. Ann grew up in Fort Smith, Arkansas, and lives in Chicago, Illinois.

**About the
Map Illustrator
Matt Kania**

Matt Kania loves maps and, as a kid, dreamed of making them. In school he studied geography and cartography, and today he makes maps for a living. Matt's favorite thing about drawing maps is learning about the places they represent. Many of the maps he has created can be found in books, magazines, videos, Web sites, and public places.

On the cover: Enjoy the natural beauty of Roger Williams Park.
On page one: Visit Prospect Park for a great view of Providence!

OUR RHODE ISLAND TRIP

Rhode Island's Nicknames:
Little Rhody and the Ocean State

WELCOME TO RHODE ISLAND

How about a trip through the Ocean State? That's Rhode Island! It may be a tiny state. But you'll find it's chock-full of adventures.

You'll dress up like someone from the 1700s. You'll watch a water mill at work. You'll see the silliest boats you can imagine. You'll spot bushes shaped like your favorite animals. You'll sail through the air on a merry-go-round. You'll gaze up at lighthouses. And you'll see ocean waves crashing ashore.

How's that for an exciting ride? Now, settle in and buckle up tight. We're off to see Rhode Island!

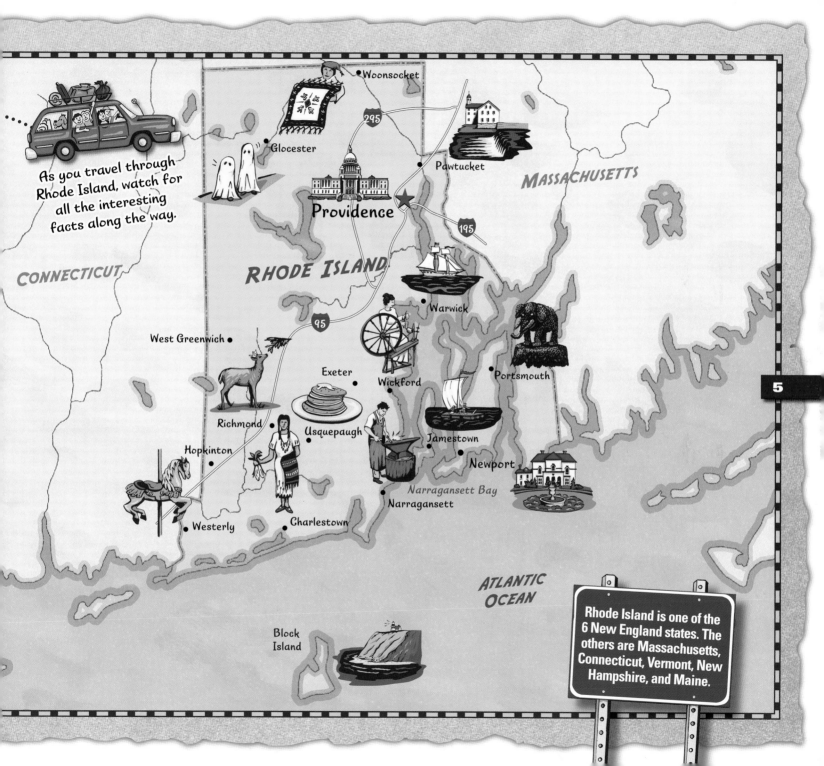

As you travel through Rhode Island, watch for all the interesting facts along the way.

Woonsocket

Glocester

Pawtucket

MASSACHUSETTS

CONNECTICUT

Providence

295

195

RHODE ISLAND

95

Warwick

West Greenwich

Exeter

Wickford

Portsmouth

Richmond

Usquepaugh

Hopkinton

Jamestown

Newport

Narragansett Bay

Westerly

Charlestown

Narragansett

ATLANTIC OCEAN

Block Island

5

Rhode Island is one of the 6 New England states. The others are Massachusetts, Connecticut, Vermont, New Hampshire, and Maine.

Enjoy the view from Mohegan Bluffs.
You might even see a ship sail by!

The southern tip of Conanicut Island is called Beavertail. Beavertail Lighthouse and Park are there.

Block Island's Mohegan Bluffs

Stroll along Mohegan Bluffs on Block Island. Waves crash on the rocks far below you. Here and there, tall lighthouses rise. All around you are sweeping views of the sea.

Tiny Rhode Island is the smallest state. It has miles of coastline, though. Narragansett Bay almost cuts the state in two. This bay flows into the Atlantic Ocean. Some coastal areas are rocky. Others have sandy beaches.

Dozens of islands lie in the bay. The largest is Aquidneck Island. Next in size are Conanicut and Prudence islands.

Block Island lies south of the **mainland.** From there, you see miles of ocean. No wonder Rhode Island is called the Ocean State!

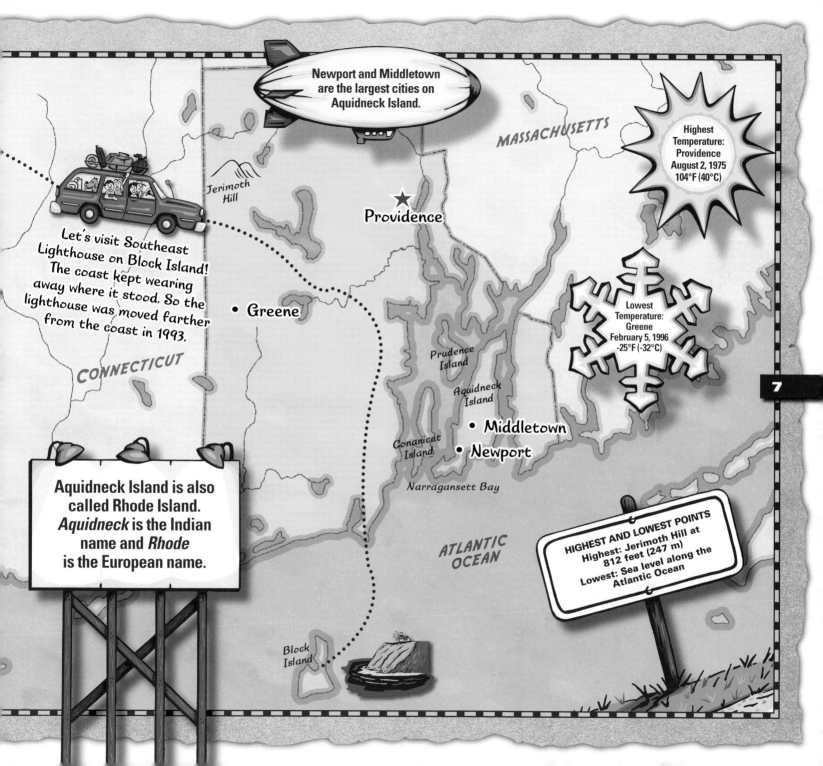

Newport and Middletown are the largest cities on Aquidneck Island.

MASSACHUSETTS

Highest Temperature: Providence August 2, 1975 104°F (40°C)

Jerimoth Hill

★ Providence

Let's visit Southeast Lighthouse on Block Island! The coast kept wearing away where it stood. So the lighthouse was moved farther from the coast in 1993.

• Greene

Lowest Temperature: Greene February 5, 1996 -25°F (-32°C)

CONNECTICUT

Prudence Island

Aquidneck Island

• Middletown

Conanicut Island

• Newport

Narragansett Bay

Aquidneck Island is also called Rhode Island. *Aquidneck* is the Indian name and *Rhode* is the European name.

ATLANTIC OCEAN

HIGHEST AND LOWEST POINTS
Highest: Jerimoth Hill at 812 feet (247 m)
Lowest: Sea level along the Atlantic Ocean

Block Island

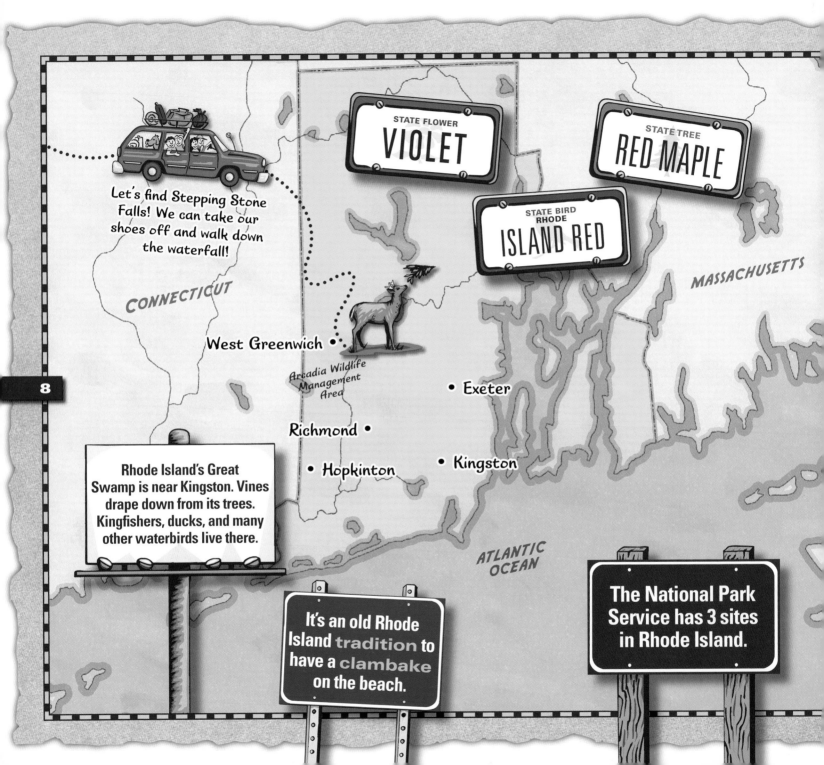

STATE FLOWER
VIOLET

STATE TREE
RED MAPLE

STATE BIRD
RHODE
ISLAND RED

Let's find Stepping Stone Falls! We can take our shoes off and walk down the waterfall!

CONNECTICUT

MASSACHUSETTS

West Greenwich •

Arcadia Wildlife Management Area

• Exeter

Richmond •

• Hopkinton

• Kingston

Rhode Island's Great Swamp is near Kingston. Vines drape down from its trees. Kingfishers, ducks, and many other waterbirds live there.

ATLANTIC OCEAN

It's an old Rhode Island **tradition** to have a **clambake** on the beach.

The National Park Service has 3 sites in Rhode Island.

Arcadia Wildlife Management Area

Sneak through the thick underbrush. You may spot a shy white-tailed deer. Do you hear rustling? It could be a raccoon or a mink. It might be a wild turkey or a pheasant. It could even be a little fox!

You're exploring Arcadia Wildlife Management Area. It's a wooded area in western Rhode Island. You'll see ponds, streams, and waterfalls there. It's a great home for forest animals.

You might spot cottontail rabbits and hawks. Gray squirrels and snowshoe hares live there, too. Frosty Hollow Pond in Exeter is a trout-fishing area. It's just for kids!

This colorful pheasant strolls through a Rhode Island meadow.

Arcadia Wildlife Management Area is spread over 4 towns. They are West Greenwich, Exeter, Hopkinton, and Richmond.

Narragansett Festivals in Charlestown

This Narragansett Indian is wearing traditional dress. He's attending a festival in Charlestown.

We celebrate Thanksgiving once a year. But the Narragansett people hold a Thanksgiving celebration every month! The grandest festival is the Green Corn Thanksgiving. It takes place in the late summer. That's when sweet corn is ripening.

Narragansett people from around the country attend. They gather on the Narragansett **reservation** in Charlestown. There they give thanks for the gift of corn.

Narragansett Indians have lived here for hundreds of years. They hunted, fished, and grew corn. Each group had a sachem, or chief. The medicine man was a spiritual guide. The Narragansett still have these leaders.

10

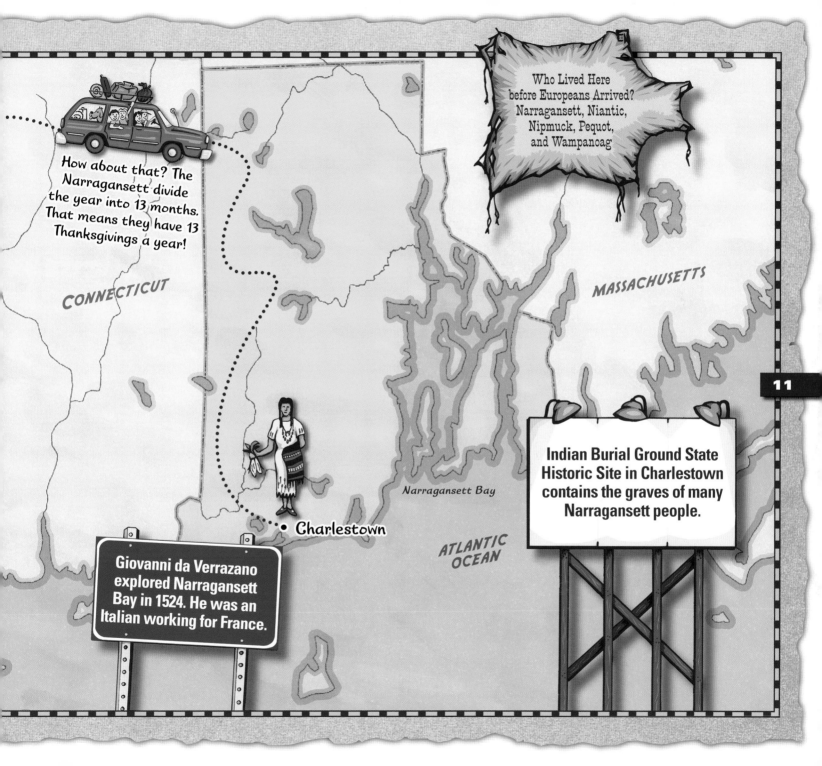

Who Lived Here before Europeans Arrived? Narragansett, Niantic, Nipmuck, Pequot, and Wampanoag

How about that? The Narragansett divide the year into 13 months. That means they have 13 Thanksgivings a year!

CONNECTICUT

MASSACHUSETTS

Narragansett Bay

Indian Burial Ground State Historic Site in Charlestown contains the graves of many Narragansett people.

• Charlestown

ATLANTIC OCEAN

Giovanni da Verrazano explored Narragansett Bay in 1524. He was an Italian working for France.

Richard Smith bought Roger Williams's trading post in 1651. Smith's house came to be called Smith's Castle.

Cool! The castle has a dye garden. Plants grown there are used to dye cloth different colors!

CONNECTICUT

MASSACHUSETTS

★ Providence

How did Rhode Island get its name? There are 3 stories. One says it was named after the Greek island of Rhodes. Another story says it was given the Dutch name *Roodt Eylandt* (meaning "Red Island") for its red soil. A third story claims Roger Williams chose the name, saying it meant "Isle of Roses."

• Portsmouth

• Wickford

Aquidneck Island

• Kingston   • Newport

People driven out of Massachusetts founded present-day Portsmouth on Aquidneck Island in 1638. Some moved south and founded Newport in 1639.

ATLANTIC OCEAN

Roger Williams founded the First Baptist Church in Providence. It's now the country's oldest Baptist church.

The Great Swamp Fight took place near Kingston in 1675. Colonists killed many Narragansett Indians in this battle.

Smith's Castle in Wickford

How did Rhode Island's first European settlers live? Just come to Opening Day at Smith's Castle! You'll see people dressed in costumes from the 1600's. They demonstrate daily life on a **plantation.**

Roger Williams's trading post once stood here. Williams established a settlement called Providence Plantations. Narragansett Indians bought goods at his trading post.

Williams first lived in the Massachusetts Bay **Colony.** This colony didn't allow religious freedom. Williams left and founded Providence in 1636. He welcomed people of all faiths. Other settlers came to Aquidneck Island. Soon a new colony was formed. It was called Rhode Island and Providence Plantations.

Want to learn what life was like in the 1600s? Just stop by Smith's Castle!

King Philip's War (1675–1676) was named after Wampanoag chief Metacom. He was called King Philip. He united several American Indian groups to drive white settlers off Indian lands. In the end, the Indians lost.

Is it a plant or an animal? See for yourself at Green Animals Topiary Garden!

Green Animals Topiary Garden in Portsmouth

Here's a big, green elephant. There's a big, green giraffe. And look at that big, green teddy bear. You're exploring Green Animals Topiary Garden!

Topiary is a fantastic art form. It's a type of sculpture. It involves trimming trees and bushes into shapes.

You'll see about eighty topiaries at Green Animals. Some are animals. And some are just beautiful shapes.

Topiary artists don't simply cut and trim. They also train branches. They carefully bend, weave, and tie them. It takes years to create a perfect shape!

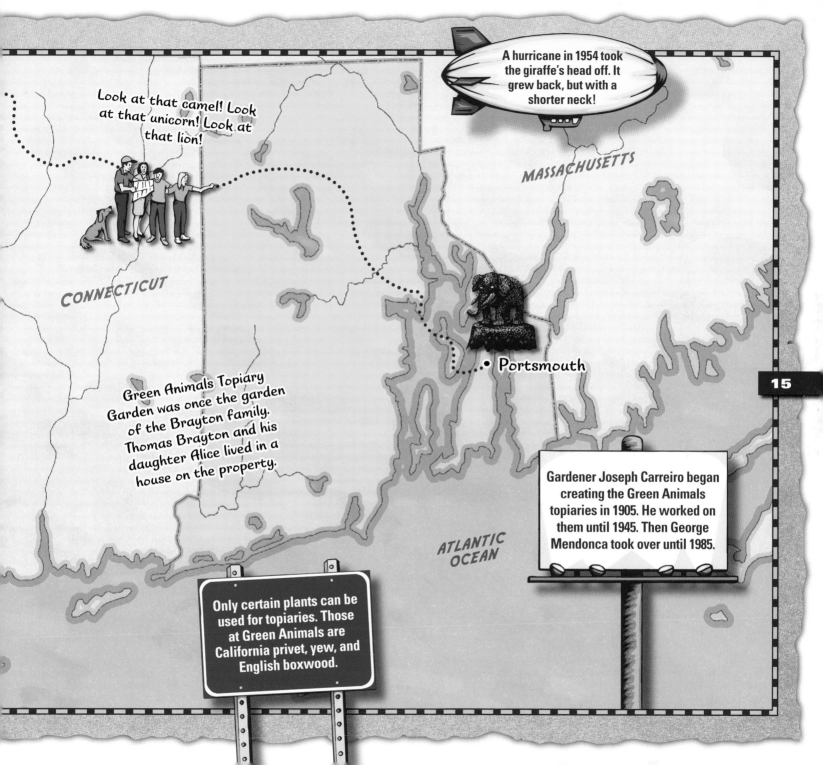

A hurricane in 1954 took the giraffe's head off. It grew back, but with a shorter neck!

Look at that camel! Look at that unicorn! Look at that lion!

MASSACHUSETTS

CONNECTICUT

Green Animals Topiary Garden was once the garden of the Brayton family. Thomas Brayton and his daughter Alice lived in a house on the property.

• Portsmouth

15

Gardener Joseph Carreiro began creating the Green Animals topiaries in 1905. He worked on them until 1945. Then George Mendonca took over until 1985.

ATLANTIC OCEAN

Only certain plants can be used for topiaries. Those at Green Animals are California privet, yew, and English boxwood.

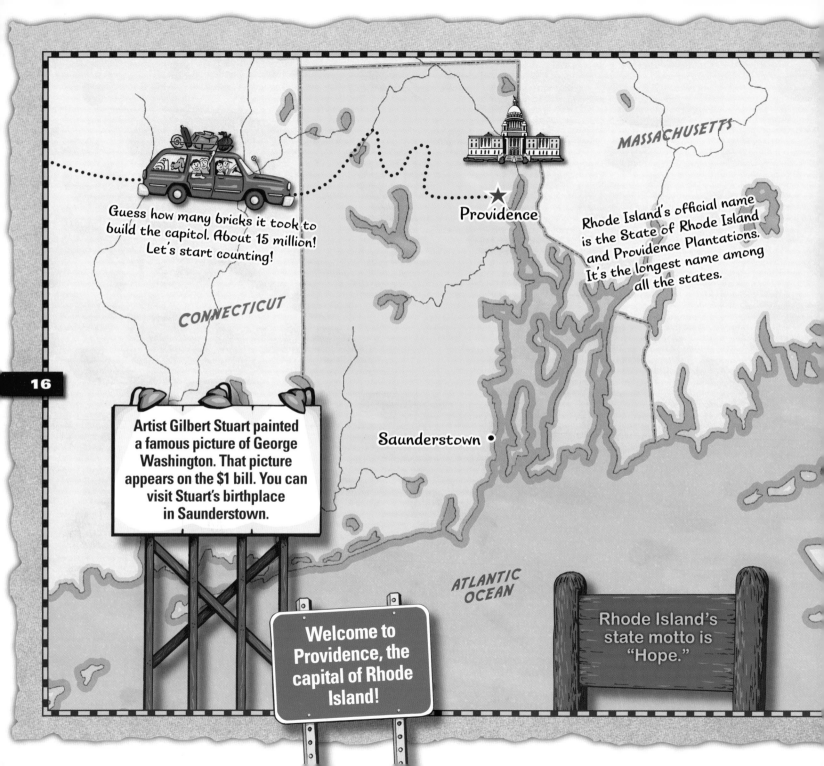

MASSACHUSETTS

Guess how many bricks it took to build the capitol. About 15 million! Let's start counting!

★
Providence

Rhode Island's official name is the State of Rhode Island and Providence Plantations. It's the longest name among all the states.

CONNECTICUT

Artist Gilbert Stuart painted a famous picture of George Washington. That picture appears on the $1 bill. You can visit Stuart's birthplace in Saunderstown.

Saunderstown •

ATLANTIC OCEAN

Welcome to Providence, the capital of Rhode Island!

Rhode Island's state motto is "Hope."

The state capitol has a massive dome. Stand beneath it and look up. It's full of huge paintings. One shows Roger Williams founding his new colony. Imagine how proud he'd be to see the capitol!

State government offices are inside this building. Rhode Island has three branches of government. One branch makes the state's laws. It's called the General Assembly. Another branch carries out the laws. The governor heads this branch. Judges make up the third branch. They apply the law to court cases. Then they decide whether laws have been broken.

Rhode Island lawmakers are busy inside the capitol.

17

Rhode Island has the 2nd-largest marble dome atop any state capitol. Only Minnesota's is larger.

Careful, that metal's hot! Watch blacksmiths work at South County Museum.

18

Only Alaska makes less money from farming than Rhode Island.

Stroll around the farmhouse and barn. People are busy with farm chores. Visit the carpenter's and blacksmith's shops. People there are hammering away.

You're touring South County Museum. It's a living history farm. Everyone's dressed in 1800s clothing. And they're happy to chat with you. They tell you what farming was like long ago.

Most early settlers had farms. They grew much of what they needed. Today, trees and shrubs are important farm products in Rhode Island. Many farmers raise cows for their milk. Some grow potatoes, hay, and other crops. Others raise chickens that lay delicious eggs!

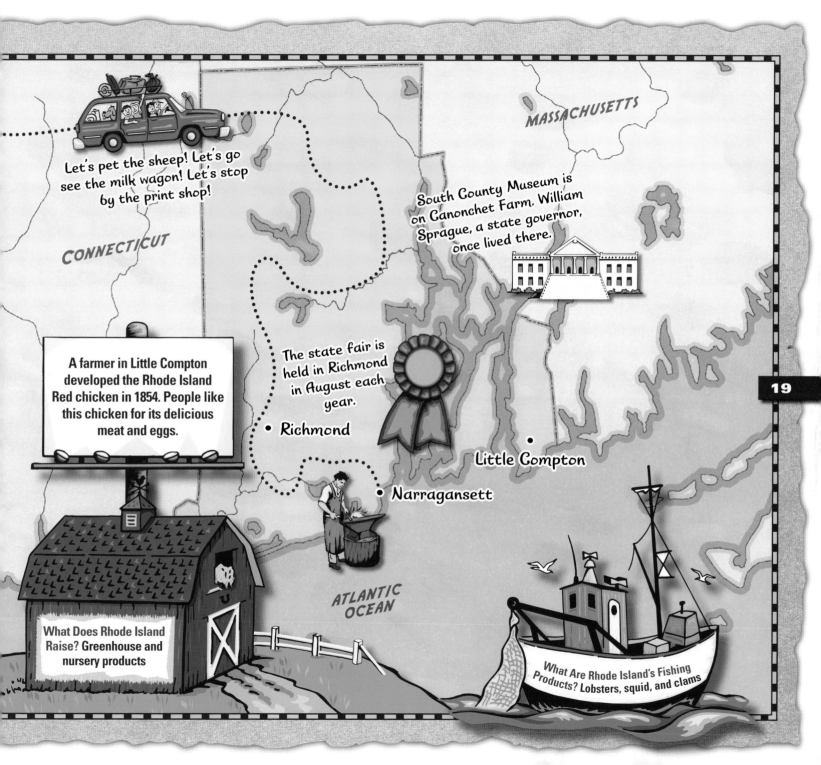

Let's pet the sheep! Let's go see the milk wagon! Let's stop by the print shop!

MASSACHUSETTS

CONNECTICUT

South County Museum is on Canonchet Farm. William Sprague, a state governor, once lived there.

A farmer in Little Compton developed the Rhode Island Red chicken in 1854. People like this chicken for its delicious meat and eggs.

The state fair is held in Richmond in August each year.

• Richmond

Little Compton

• Narragansett

What Does Rhode Island Raise? Greenhouse and nursery products

ATLANTIC OCEAN

What Are Rhode Island's Fishing Products? Lobsters, squid, and clams

19

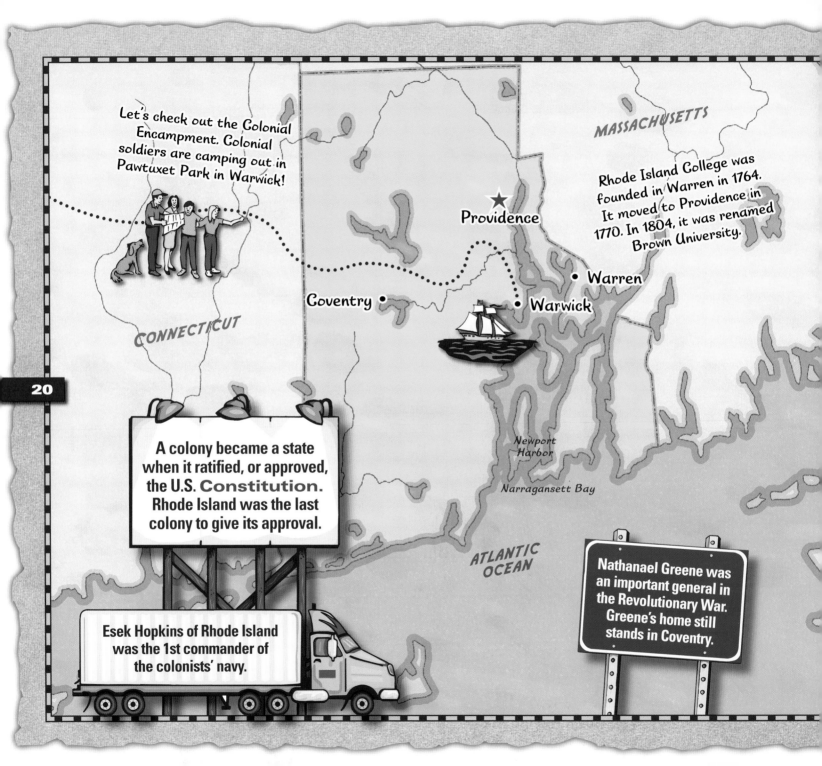

Let's check out the Colonial Encampment. Colonial soldiers are camping out in Pawtuxet Park in Warwick!

MASSACHUSETTS

Rhode Island College was founded in Warren in 1764. It moved to Providence in 1770. In 1804, it was renamed Brown University.

★ Providence

• Warren

Coventry •

• Warwick

CONNECTICUT

Newport Harbor

Narragansett Bay

A colony became a state when it ratified, or approved, the U.S. Constitution. Rhode Island was the last colony to give its approval.

ATLANTIC OCEAN

Nathanael Greene was an important general in the Revolutionary War. Greene's home still stands in Coventry.

Esek Hopkins of Rhode Island was the 1st commander of the colonists' navy.

Gaspée Days in Warwick

Rhode Island was the 13th state to enter the Union. It joined on May 29, 1790.

Stand at attention! You're watching the Pawtucket Rangers Militia at Gaspée Days.

Want to dress up like a **colonist**? Put on a three-cornered hat or long skirt. Then enter the Children's Colonial Costume Contest! It's a fun event during Warwick's Gaspée Days. This festival celebrates an exciting time in history.

Rhode Island was one of the thirteen original colonies. They were ruled by Great Britain. The colonists grew to hate Britain's high taxes.

Rhode Island colonists took action in 1772. They burned the British ship *Gaspée* in Narragansett Bay. This helped lead to the Revolutionary War (1775–1783). The colonies won! They became the first thirteen U.S. states.

In 1769, Rhode Islanders burned the British ship *Liberty* in Newport Harbor.

Ever wonder how cloth is made? Visit Slater Mill in Pawtucket to find out!

Old Slater Mill in Pawtucket

The massive wheel begins to turn. The floor vibrates as machines clank. They spin raw cotton into thread and cloth. You're watching Slater Mill in action!

Samuel Slater built this mill in 1793. It was the country's first water-powered cotton mill. Water from the Blackstone River turns its wheel.

Dozens of mills once lined the Blackstone River. They made cotton and wool textiles, or cloth. Textiles became Rhode Island's leading **industry.**

Slater Mill is a great place to visit. A mill workers' village surrounds the mill. Costumed villagers show you how the workers lived.

Samuel Slater built his 1st mill in Pawtucket in 1793. Children ages 7 to 12 worked there!

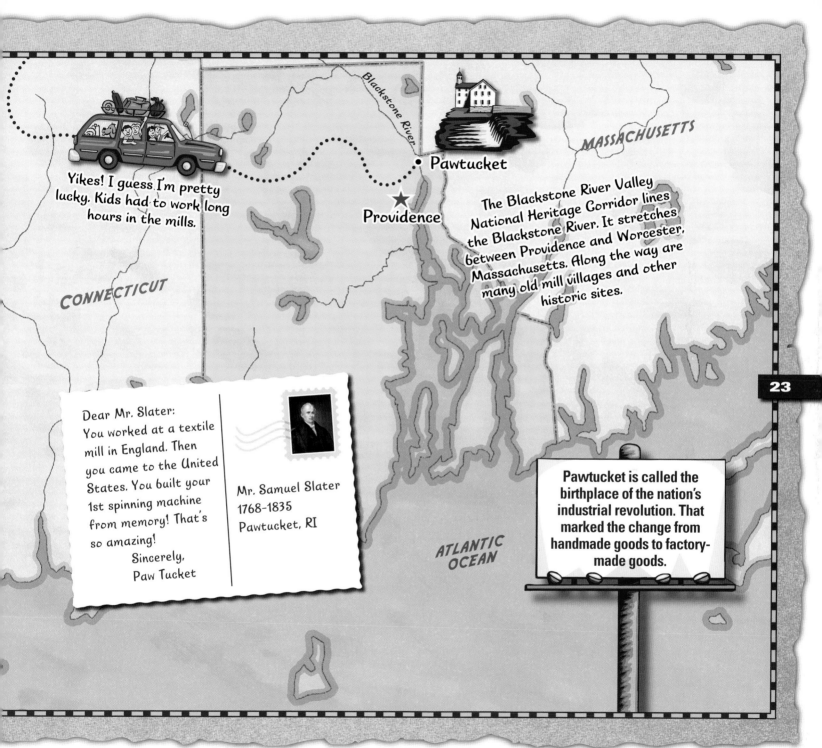

Yikes! I guess I'm pretty lucky. Kids had to work long hours in the mills.

The Blackstone River Valley National Heritage Corridor lines the Blackstone River. It stretches between Providence and Worcester, Massachusetts. Along the way are many old mill villages and other historic sites.

Pawtucket is called the birthplace of the nation's industrial revolution. That marked the change from handmade goods to factory-made goods.

Dear Mr. Slater:
You worked at a textile mill in England. Then you came to the United States. You built your 1st spinning machine from memory! That's so amazing!
　　　　Sincerely,
　　　　Paw Tucket

Mr. Samuel Slater
1768–1835
Pawtucket, RI

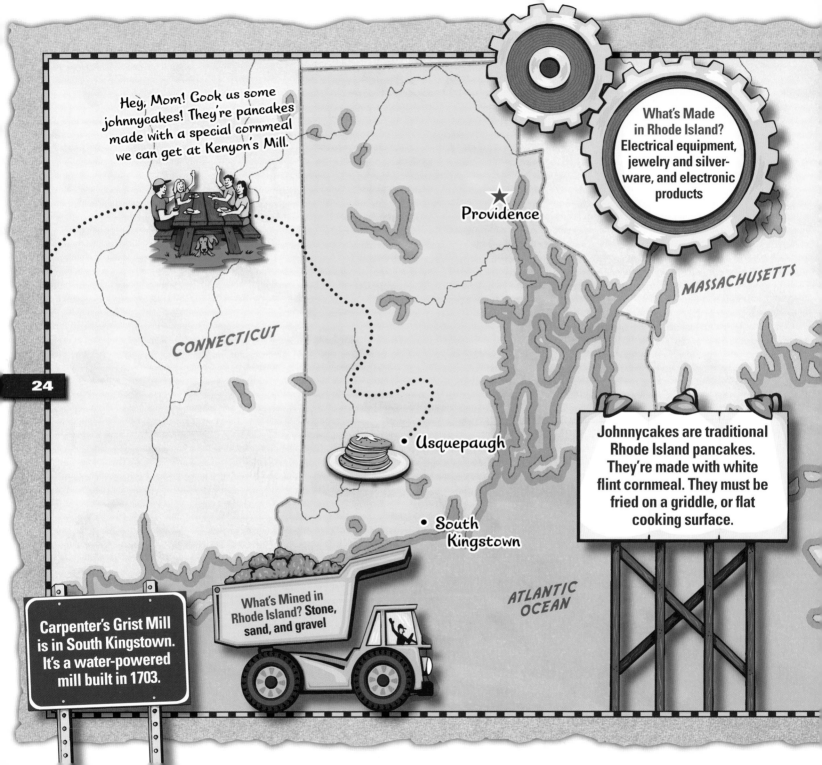

Hey, Mom! Cook us some johnnycakes! They're pancakes made with a special cornmeal we can get at Kenyon's Mill.

MASSACHUSETTS

★
Providence

CONNECTICUT

• Usquepaugh

• South Kingstown

Johnnycakes are traditional Rhode Island pancakes. They're made with white flint cornmeal. They must be fried on a griddle, or flat cooking surface.

ATLANTIC OCEAN

Carpenter's Grist Mill is in South Kingstown. It's a water-powered mill built in 1703.

What's Mined in Rhode Island? Stone, sand, and gravel

Kenyon's Grist Mill in Usquepaugh

Textile mills weren't Rhode Island's only mills. There were lots of grist mills, too. These were mills that ground grain. Corn or wheat was poured in. A huge stone ground up the grain. Then out came cornmeal or flour!

How did it all work? Just visit Kenyon's Grist Mill. It dates back to the early 1700s. It's still grinding grain the old-fashioned way.

Rhode Island has powerful factories now. Some make electrical equipment or computer products. Others make machines, tools, or plastics. Rhode Island is known for making jewelry, too.

Yum, you can smell the johnnycakes cooking! Don't forget to stop by Kenyon's Grist Mill!

Rhode Islanders flock to this waterfront festival in Providence.

The Ancients and Horribles Parade

Check out the Ancients and Horribles Parade! It's held in Glocester every Fourth of July. People wear the wildest, ugliest outfits they can come up with. They decorate their cars, trucks, and bikes. Each vehicle looks really wacky, too.

Rhode Islanders find lots of ways to have fun. They hold parades, sailboat races, and fishing contests. They attend seafood festivals and clambakes. There's plenty to do along the shore. People enjoy swimming, boating, and fishing.

May Breakfasts are traditional events. They're served around the state in May. Johnnycakes are usually on the menu!

Bristol claims to have the nation's oldest 4th of July celebration. It was first held in 1785.

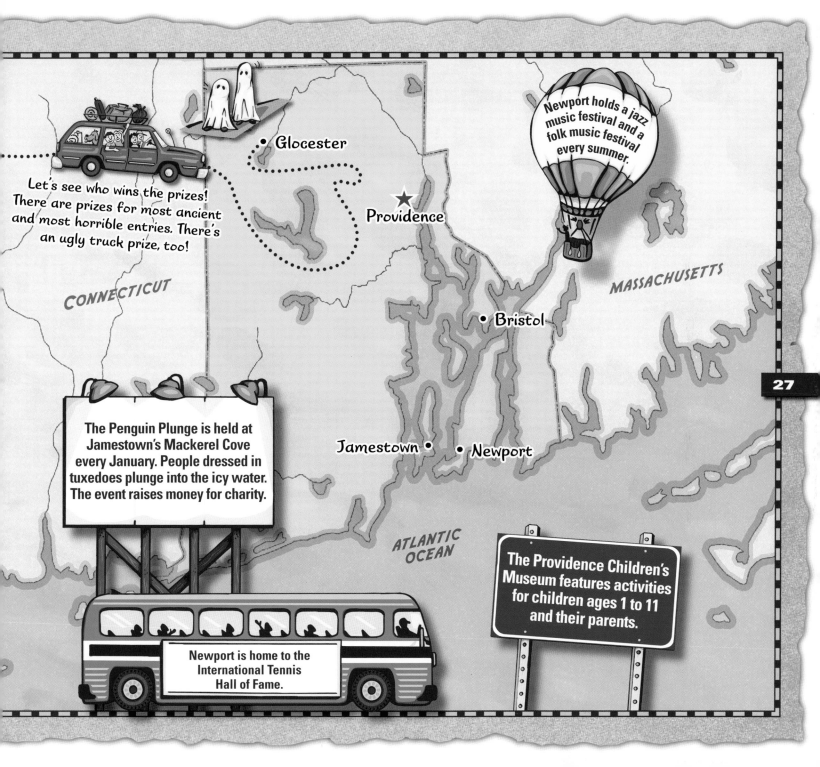

Let's see who wins the prizes! There are prizes for most ancient and most horrible entries. There's an ugly truck prize, too!

• Glocester

★ Providence

Newport holds a jazz music festival and a folk music festival every summer.

CONNECTICUT

MASSACHUSETTS

• Bristol

The Penguin Plunge is held at Jamestown's Mackerel Cove every January. People dressed in tuxedoes plunge into the icy water. The event raises money for charity.

Jamestown • • Newport

ATLANTIC OCEAN

The Providence Children's Museum features activities for children ages 1 to 11 and their parents.

Newport is home to the International Tennis Hall of Fame.

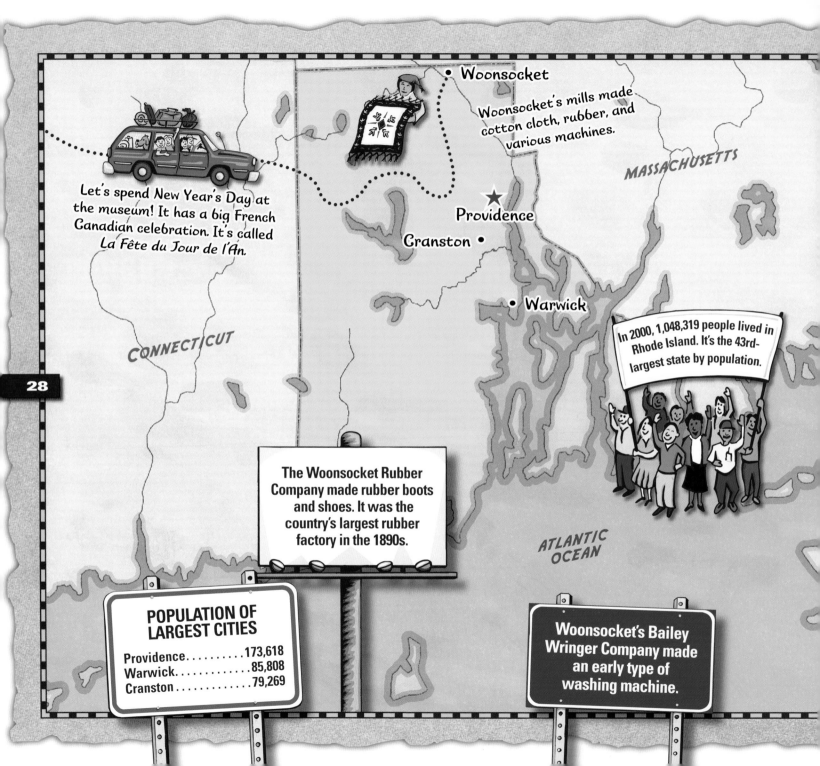

Let's spend New Year's Day at the museum! It has a big French Canadian celebration. It's called La Fête du Jour de l'An.

Woonsocket's mills made cotton cloth, rubber, and various machines.

In 2000, 1,048,319 people lived in Rhode Island. It's the 43rd-largest state by population.

The Woonsocket Rubber Company made rubber boots and shoes. It was the country's largest rubber factory in the 1890s.

POPULATION OF LARGEST CITIES

Providence 173,618
Warwick 85,808
Cranston 79,269

Woonsocket's Bailey Wringer Company made an early type of washing machine.

MASSACHUSETTS
CONNECTICUT
ATLANTIC OCEAN

Woonsocket
Providence
Cranston
Warwick

The French Canadians of Woonsocket

In 1900, about 7 out of 10 Rhode Islanders were born outside the United States.

Stroll through a millworker's living room. Hear workers chat in a textile mill. Visit a school classroom from the 1920s.

You're at Woonsocket's Museum of Work and Culture. It's all about the city's French Canadian **immigrants.** You can walk right through the displays!

French Canadians are Woonsocket's largest **ethnic** group. Thousands of them arrived in the 1800s. They came from Canada's Quebec province. They went to work in Woonsocket's mills.

Many other immigrant groups moved to Rhode Island. They came from Italy, Portugal, Sweden, and Poland.

Would you have made a good millworker? Visit Woonsocket to find out!

Would you like to live here? The butler awaits you at the Astors' Beechwood.

Cliff Walk is a high seaside walking path in Newport. It passes many mansions.

The Astors' Beechwood and Other Newport Mansions

Walk up the grand staircase. An elegant lady may be fluttering her fan. Sneak into the servants' rooms. You might hear some juicy gossip!

You're touring the Astors' Beechwood. It's a glittering mansion in Newport. And you're taking a peek into another time. Costumed actors are bustling here and there. They're playing the roles of family, friends, and servants.

You can tour several of the Newport mansions. Wealthy people built them in the late 1800s. Many of the owners lived in New York most of the year. The Newport mansions were just their summer homes!

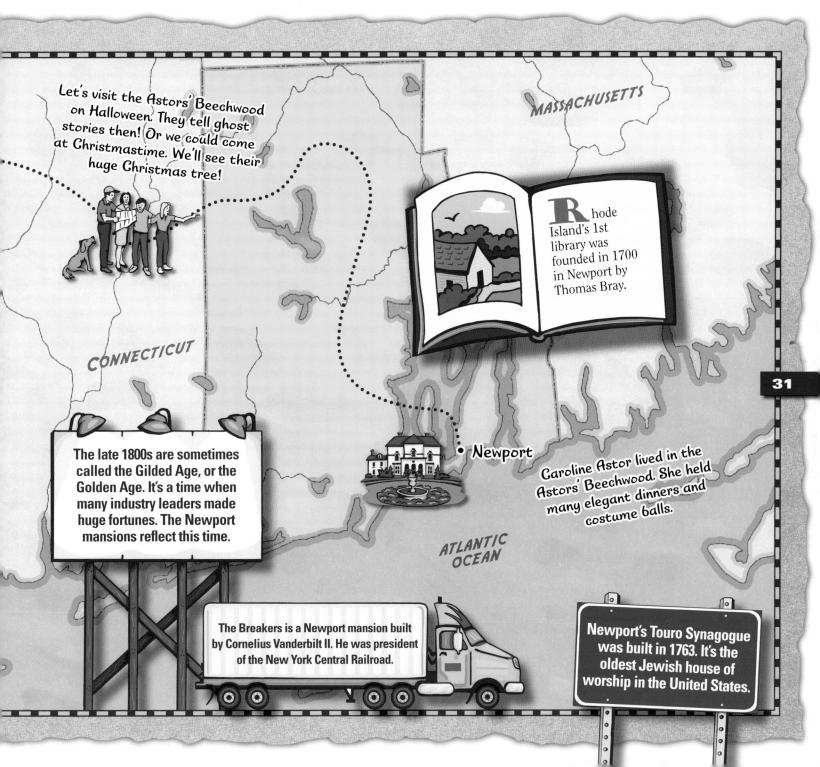

Let's visit the Astors' Beechwood on Halloween. They tell ghost stories then! Or we could come at Christmastime. We'll see their huge Christmas tree!

MASSACHUSETTS

Rhode Island's 1st library was founded in 1700 in Newport by Thomas Bray.

CONNECTICUT

• Newport

The late 1800s are sometimes called the Gilded Age, or the Golden Age. It's a time when many industry leaders made huge fortunes. The Newport mansions reflect this time.

Caroline Astor lived in the Astors' Beechwood. She held many elegant dinners and costume balls.

ATLANTIC OCEAN

The Breakers is a Newport mansion built by Cornelius Vanderbilt II. He was president of the New York Central Railroad.

Newport's Touro Synagogue was built in 1763. It's the oldest Jewish house of worship in the United States.

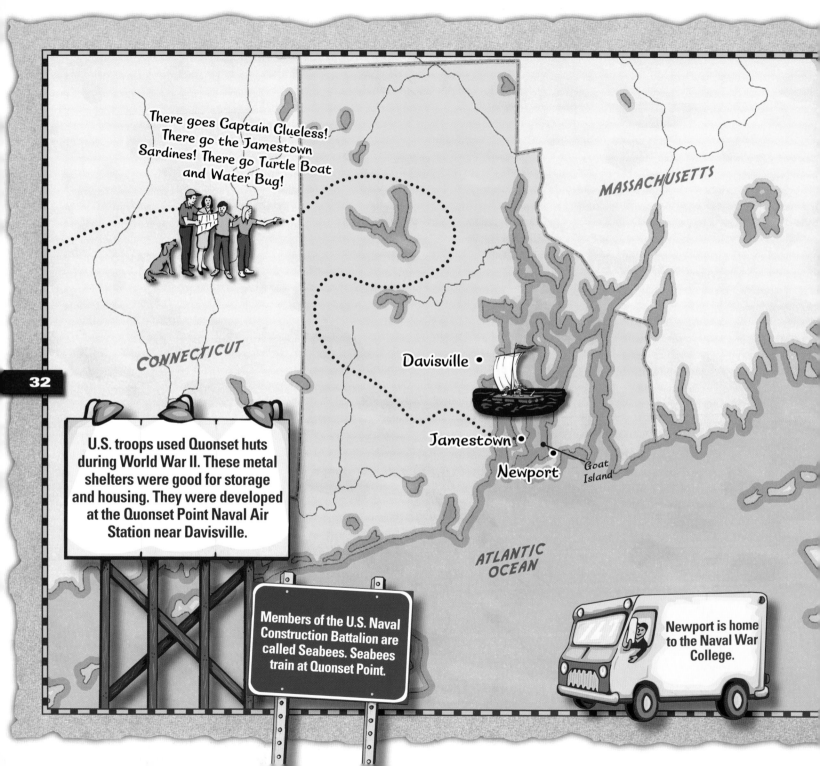

There goes Captain Clueless! There go the Jamestown Sardines! There go Turtle Boat and Water Bug!

MASSACHUSETTS

CONNECTICUT

Davisville •

Jamestown •

Newport •

Goat Island

ATLANTIC OCEAN

U.S. troops used Quonset huts during World War II. These metal shelters were good for storage and housing. They were developed at the Quonset Point Naval Air Station near Davisville.

Members of the U.S. Naval Construction Battalion are called Seabees. Seabees train at Quonset Point.

Newport is home to the Naval War College.

The Fools' Rules Regatta in Jamestown

Boom! The cannon fires, and people start to work. They have two hours to build their sailboats. They might use doghouses or sandboxes. They might use car parts or chicken cages. They name their boats, and then the race begins. It's the Fools' Rules **Regatta**!

This is a race for really silly boats. Rhode Island has many serious sailboat races, too. It also has many ties with the U.S. Navy.

A **torpedo** factory opened on Goat Island in 1906. Rhode Island built warships during World War I (1914–1918). The state was also busy during World War II (1939–1945). Thousands of navy troops trained there.

The Naval Undersea Warfare Center is in Newport.

Ready, set, go! Racers build their boats for the Fools' Rules Regatta.

Thousands of sailors trained at Newport's Naval Training Station during World War II.

34

Want to ride a flying horse in Westerly?
Just saddle up and hold on tight!

Only children are allowed to ride the Flying Horse Carousel.

Westerly's Flying Horse Carousel

Whee! You're riding a carousel, or merry-go-round. And you're not just moving up and down. You're sailing through the air! You're riding the Flying Horse Carousel. It dates from the 1870s.

These carousel horses are hand-carven from wood. Their manes and tails are real horse hair. They wear leather saddles. And their eyes seem to sparkle! They're made of a stone called agate.

Why is this called the Flying Horse Carousel? The horses aren't attached to the floor. They only hang from above. When the carousel turns, the horses swing outward. The faster the ride, the farther they swing. They really seem to fly!

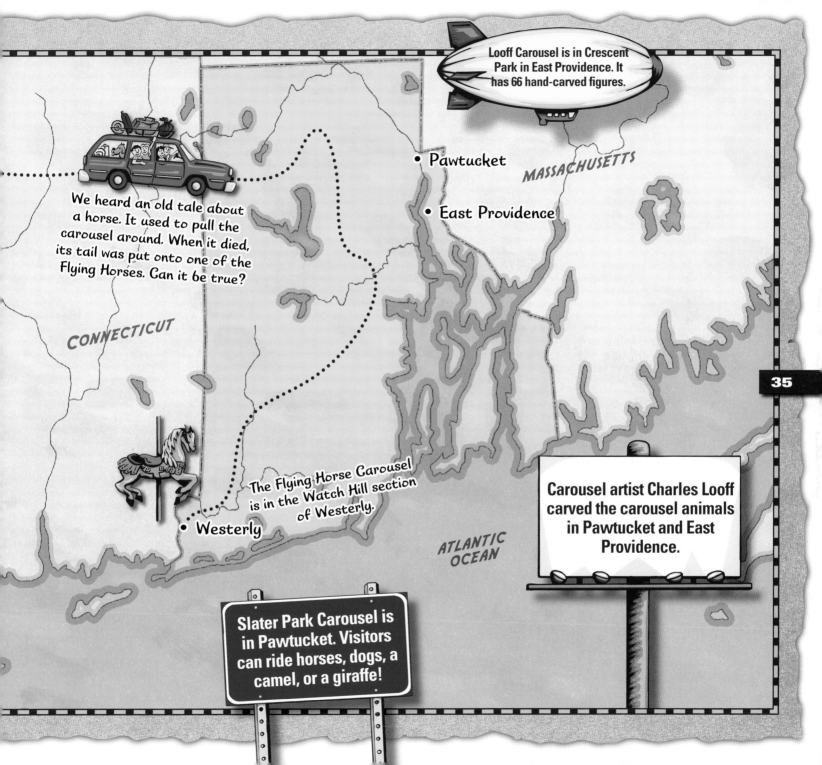

Looff Carousel is in Crescent Park in East Providence. It has 66 hand-carved figures.

• Pawtucket

MASSACHUSETTS

• East Providence

We heard an old tale about a horse. It used to pull the carousel around. When it died, its tail was put onto one of the Flying Horses. Can it be true?

CONNECTICUT

The Flying Horse Carousel is in the Watch Hill section of Westerly.

• Westerly

ATLANTIC OCEAN

Carousel artist Charles Looff carved the carousel animals in Pawtucket and East Providence.

Slater Park Carousel is in Pawtucket. Visitors can ride horses, dogs, a camel, or a giraffe!

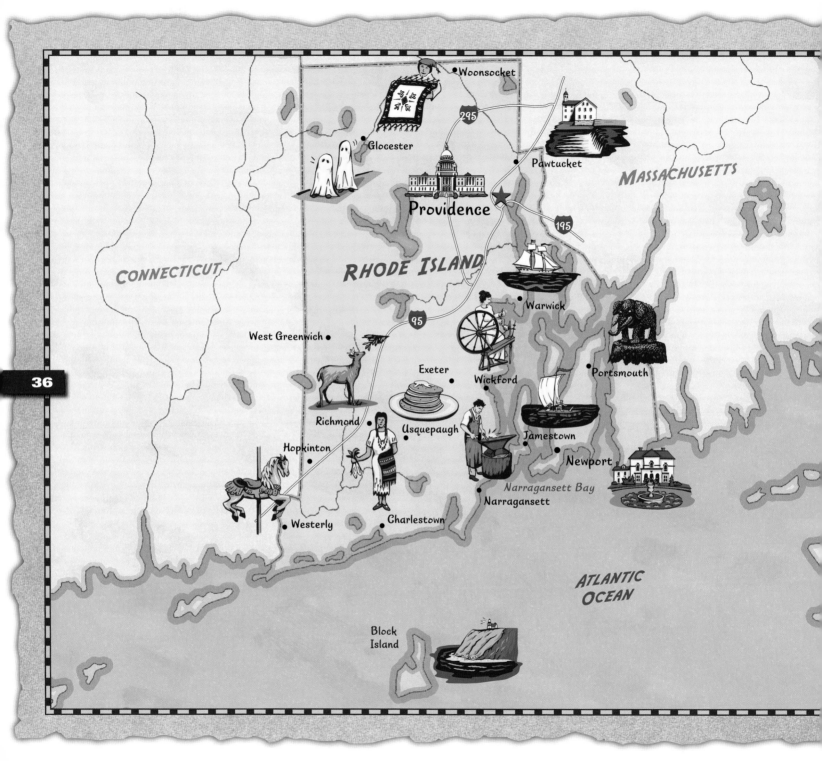

Woonsocket

Glocester

295

Pawtucket

MASSACHUSETTS

Providence

CONNECTICUT

RHODE ISLAND

195

Warwick

West Greenwich

Exeter

Wickford

Portsmouth

95

Richmond

Usquepaugh

Jamestown

Hopkinton

Newport

Narragansett Bay

Narragansett

Westerly

Charlestown

ATLANTIC
OCEAN

Block
Island

OUR TRIP

We visited many amazing places on our trip! We also met a lot of interesting people along the way. Look at the map on the left. Use your finger to trace all the places we have been.

What are the 6 New England states? See page 5 for the answer.

What is another name for Aquidneck Island? Page 7 has the answer.

When did the Great Swamp Fight take place? See page 12 for the answer.

What are some plants that can be used in topiaries? Look on page 15 for the answer.

What was Brown University once called? Page 20 has the answer.

What are johnnycakes? Turn to page 24 for the answer.

When was Newport's Touro Synagogue built? Look on page 31 for the answer.

Who carved the carousel animals in Pawtucket and East Providence? Turn to page 35 for the answer.

That was a great trip! We have traveled all over Rhode Island!
There are a few places we didn't have time for, though. Next time, we plan to visit Roger Williams Park Zoo in Providence. Visitors can see more than 1,000 animals, including polar bears, giraffes, and snow leopards. Kids learn about various endangered animals and what they can do to help them.

More Places to Visit in Rhode Island

WORDS TO KNOW

clambake (KLAM-bake) a beach party where clams are cooked

colonist (KOL-uh-nist) someone who settles a new land for his or her home country

colony (KOL-uh-nee) a land settled and governed by another country

constitution (kon-stuh-TOO-shuhn) the basic set of ideas and laws for a country or state

ethnic (ETH-nik) relating to a person's race or nationality

immigrants (IM-uh-gruhnts) people who move to another country

industry (IN-duh-stree) a type of business

mainland (MAYN-luhnd) land that makes up the main part of a state or country

plantation (plan-TAY-shuhn) a large farm that raises mainly 1 crop

regatta (ri-GAT-uh) a boat race

reservation (rez-ur-VAY-shuhn) land set aside for a special use, such as for Native Americans

torpedo (tor-PEE-doh) a missile that's fired underwater

tradition (truh-DISH-uhn) a long-held custom

Rhode Island covers 1,045 square miles (2,607 sq km). It's the 50th-largest state in size.

STATE SYMBOLS

State bird: Rhode Island Red (a chicken)

State drink: Coffee milk

State fish: Striped bass

State flagship: Continental schooner *Providence*

State flower: Violet

State fruit: Rhode Island greening (an apple)

State mineral: Bowenite

State rock: Cumberlandite

State shell: Quahog

State tree: Red maple

State yacht: *Courageous*

State flag

State seal

STATE SONG

"Rhode Island's It for Me"

Words by Charlie Hall, music by Maria Day

I've been to every state we have,
and I think that I'm inclined to say
that Rhody stole my heart:
You can keep the forty-nine.

Herring gulls that dot the sky,
blue waves that paint the rocks,
waters rich with Neptune's life,
the boats that line the docks,
I see the lighthouse flickering
to help the sailors see.
There's a place for everyone:
Rhode Island's it for me.

Chorus:
Rhode Island, oh, Rhode Island
surrounded by the sea.
Some people roam the earth for home;
Rhode Island's it for me.

I love the fresh October days,
the buzz of College Hill,
art that moves an eye to tear,
a jeweler's special skill.
Icicles refract the sun,
snow falling gracefully.
Some search for a place that's w
Rhode Island's it for me.

(Chorus)

The skyline piercing Providence,
the State House dome so rare,
residents who speak their minds;
no longer unaware!
Roger Williams would be proud
to see his colony,
so don't sell short this precious p
Rhode Island's it for me.

FAMOUS PEOPLE

Burnside, Ambrose Everett (1824–1881), Civil War general, governor of Rhode Island

Cohan, George M. (1878–1942), entertainer

Colasanto, Nicholas (1924–1985), actor and director

Gray, Robert (1755–1806), sea captain

Gray, Spalding (1941–2004), actor and writer

Hackett, Bobby (1915–1976), jazz musician

Howe, Julia Ward (1819–1910), writer and reformer

Hussey, Ruth (1914–), actor

Hutchinson, Anne (1591–1643), religious leader

Kinnell, Galway (1927–), poet

Lajoie, Napoleon (1874–1959), baseball player

Lovecraft, H. P. (1890–1937), author

Macaulay, David (1946–), children's author and illustrator

Massasoit (ca. 1580–1661), American Indian chief

Perry, Mathew C. (1794–1858), U.S. Navy officer

Perry, Oliver Hazard (1785–1819), U.S. Navy officer and war hero

Slater, Samuel (1768–1835), founder of the U.S. textile industry

Stuart, Gilbert Charles (1755–1828), painter

Van Allsburg, Chris (1949–), children's author and illustrator

Williams, Roger (ca. 1603–1683), founder of Rhode Island

Woodcock, Leonard (1911–2001), labor leader

TO FIND OUT MORE

At the Library

Curtis, Alice Turner, and Wuanita Smith (illustrator). *A Little Maid of Narragansett Bay.* Bedford, Mass.: Applewood Books, 1998.

Holtzman, Robert, and Wayne Marcus (illustrator). *Boats and Ships of Rhode Island: Your Field Guide.* North Kingstown, R.I.: Moon Mountain Publishing, 2004.

Somervill, Barbara A. *The Rhode Island Colony.* Chanhassen, Minn.: The Child's World, 2003.

Walsh, Kiernan. *Roger Williams.* Vero Beach, Fla.: Rourke Pub., 2004.

On the Web

Visit our home page for lots of links about Rhode Island:
http://www.childsworld.com/links

Note to Parents, Teachers, and Librarians: We routinely verify our Web links to make sure they are safe, active sites—so encourage your readers to check them out!

Places to Visit or Contact

Rhode Island Historical Society
110 Benevolent Street
Providence, RI 02906
401/331-8575
For more information about the history of Rhode Island

Rhode Island Tourism Division
One West Exchange Street
Providence, RI 02903
800/556-2484
For more information about traveling in Rhode Island

INDEX

Bye, Ocean State.
We had a great time.
We'll come back soon!